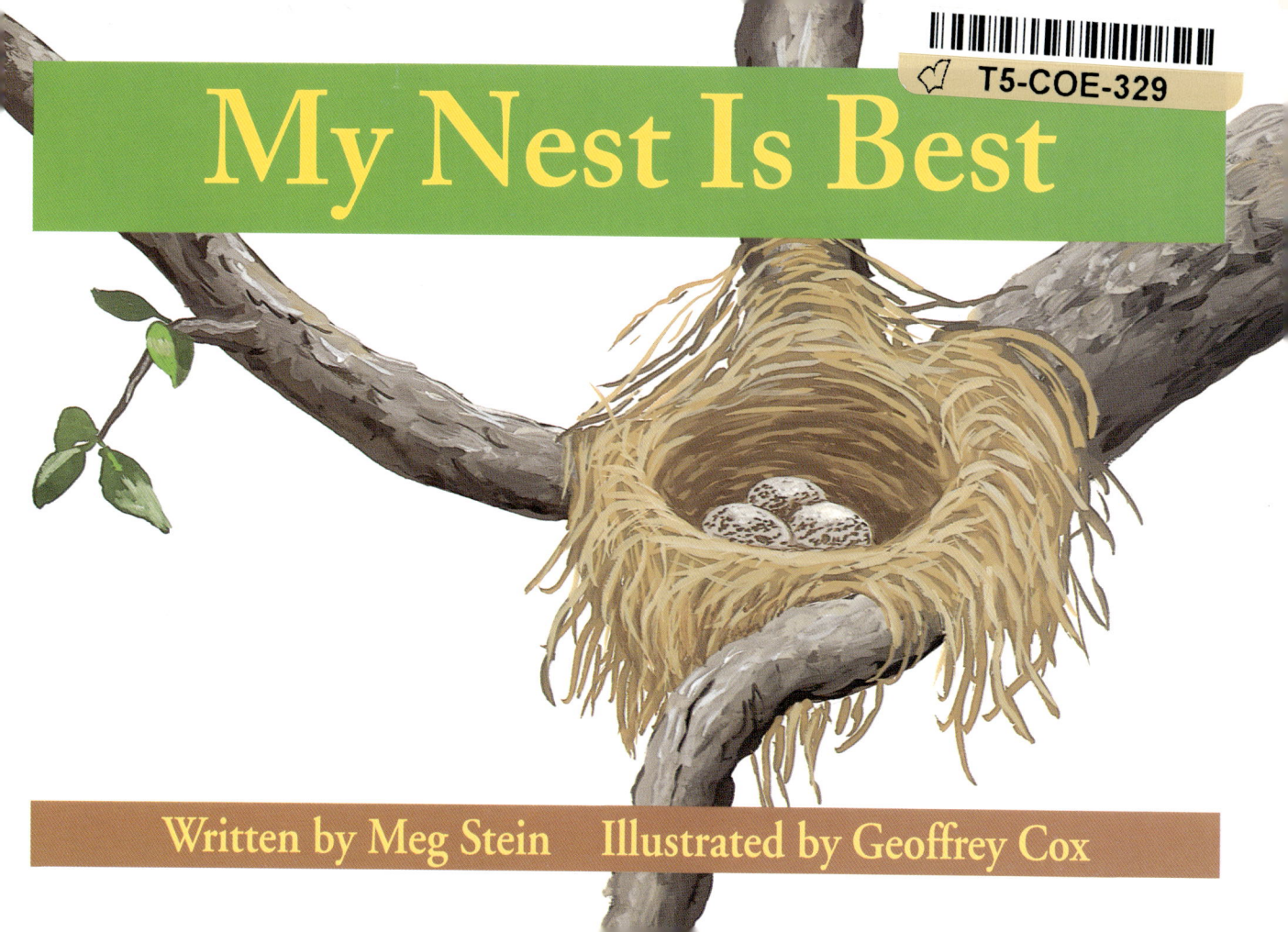

My Nest Is Best

Written by Meg Stein   Illustrated by Geoffrey Cox

"My nest is best,"
said the sparrow.
"It is up on a branch."

3

"My nest is best,"
said the ant.
"It is down under the ground."

5

"My nest is best,"
said the hen.
"It is out in the yard."

7

"My nest is best," said the wasp.
"It is up on the wall."

9

"My nest is best,"
said the duck.
"It is near the shed."

11

"My nest is best,"
said the bee.
"It is up in a tree."

13

"No, my nest is best," said the eagle.
"It is high up on a mountain."

15

16